How To ~~Pass~~ Blitz! ABRSM Theory
Grade 5

by Samantha Coates

ISBN: 978-1-78558-939-3

Chester Music

Copyright © 2018 Chester Music, a part of HAL LEONARD LLC
International Copyright Secured All Rights Reserved

No part of this publication may be reproduced in any form or by
any means without the prior written permission of the Publisher.

Visit Hal Leonard Online at
www.halleonard.com

Contact us:
Hal Leonard
7777 West Bluemound Road
Milwaukee, WI 53213
Email: info@halleonard.com

In Europe, contact:
Hal Leonard Europe Limited
42 Wigmore Street
Marylebone, London, W1U 2RY
Email: info@halleonardeurope.com

In Australia, contact:
Hal Leonard Australia Pty. Ltd.
4 Lentara Court
Cheltenham, Victoria, 3192 Australia
Email: info@halleonard.com.au

A Note From the Author

Dear theory student,

Congratulations! You have just done the very best thing for your theory education — you've bought this book. Not only that, this edition reflects the changes in the 2018 syllabus, so it covers everything you need to know and nothing you don't!

There are quite a lot of new things to learn in Grade 5, but what you really need to know is that this book builds on the knowledge you gained in Grades 1–4. If you are 'jumping in' at Grade 5 level because you have a practical exam coming up, there will be many things you need to brush up on. All of this is outlined on page 5, but the best strategy is to work through the workbooks from previous grades before you start this book. Discuss this more with your teacher, of course.

Every time you see this icon: it means there are extra resources available on the website.

Go to www.blitzbooks.com to download free worksheets, flashcards, manuscript and more!

Happy theory-ing,

Samantha

It takes more than an author and a publisher to produce a book — it takes enormous support from friends and family. Thank you to everyone who has helped me on the BlitzBooks journey, but most of all to Andrew, Thomas and Courtney... without you three, there would simply be no books.

Contents

New Keys 6

Tenor Clef 10

Irregular Time Signatures and Divisions 12

Compound Intervals 16

Transposing Instruments 22

Transposing Tricks 26

A Bit of Revision 29

Chord II and Inversions 30

Identifying Chords 33

SATB: Vocal Ranges 35

Short Test 36

Another Short Test 37

Cadences 38

More About Cadences 39

Ornaments 42

Repetitions and Repeats 43

Quick Quiz 44

Italian and German Terms 45

Tiny Test 46

Instrument Families 47

Crossword 52

Use Your Skills 54

Test Paper... Sort Of 58

Things You Should Know From Grades 1-4

You'll need to do a crash course on this stuff with your teacher if you are jumping in at Grade 5 level! (The best way to do this, of course, is to work through How to Blitz! ABRSM Theory Grades 1-4)

KEY SIGNATURES: Major and minor keys with up to five sharps or flats, and the major and minor scales of these keys, as well as chromatic scales starting on any note.

TIME SIGNATURES: All simple and compound time signatures.

NOTE VALUES: All note and rest values from breve down to demisemiquaver, double-dotted notes, duplets, and the correct groupings of notes and rests within time signatures.

TERMINOLOGY: Names of ornaments, technical scale degree names, e.g. supertonic.

CLEFS: Recognising notes in the ALTO clef (in addition to treble and bass).

OTHER STUFF: You'll also need to know how to go about any of the following tasks, because these could easily crop up in your Grade 5 exam!

★ Write major, minor (both forms) or chromatic scales in any of the set keys/clefs

★ Rewrite melodies in any of the set clefs either at the same pitch or up/down an octave, sometimes converting from accidentals to key signature and vice versa

★ Fix beaming and grouping in rhythmic exercises containing errors

★ Rewrite melodies with notes of half or twice the value

★ Convert rhythms from simple to compound and vice versa

★ Write and recognise chords I, IV and V in root position in any of the set keys/clefs

★ Name any interval by number and type, including diminished and augmented intervals

★ Answer general questions about standard orchestral instruments

★ Recognise ornaments and signs, and translate all the Italian (and French) terms you learned in Grades 1-4! (These can be downloaded from **www.blitzbooks.com**)

Got all that? Woo hoo you're ready to tackle Grade 5! Turn the page!

New Sharp Keys

Our new sharp keys for Grade 5 are F# major and its relative D# minor. These keys have SIX sharps! Here is the key signature in the treble clef. Rewrite it in bass and alto clefs:

  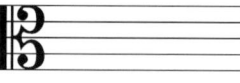

You'll remember from Grade 4 that G# minor needed a **double sharp** (𝄪) to raise the leading note. Well, D# minor is the same:

Look! The 7th note is already a C sharp! Add a double sharp here

Write a D# melodic minor scale below, using semibreves. Write the key signature, and write one octave ascending and descending. (You'll need to use a single sharp to cancel the double sharp on the way down.)

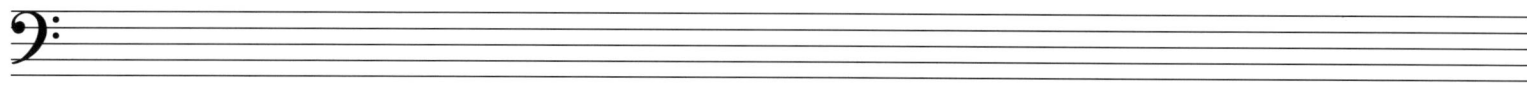

Now write an F# major scale, one octave descending, using accidentals instead of a key signature (also in semibreves). Check the clef!

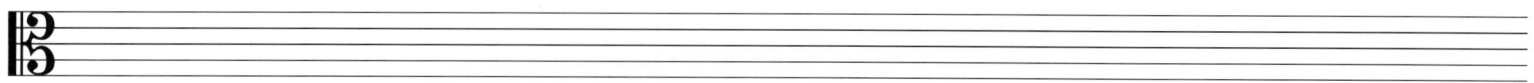

Write these key signatures and scale degrees (again, in semibreves). Watch out for clef changes!

B major
supertonic

A major
submediant

C# minor
subdominant

D# minor
leading note

Write the tonic (I), subdominant (IV) and dominant (V) triads in root position in our two new keys with six sharps in the key signature. Check the clefs, and don't forget to raise the leading note in chord V of D# minor!

F# major   D# minor

Here is a melody with lots of sharps.

Beethoven

What key is it in? (Hint: bar 1 centres around the tonic, and the melody contains E sharps.) _____

Rewrite the melody here, using a key signature instead of accidentals:

Name this scale:

For your final trick using sharps, write a one-octave ascending **chromatic** scale beginning on F#. Use semibreves, and write the scale in any clef you like!

New Flat Keys

Our new flat keys for Grade 5 are G♭ major and E♭ minor. These keys have SIX flats! Here is the key signature in the bass clef. Rewrite it in alto and treble clefs:

Write an E♭ melodic minor scale here, using semibreves. Write the key signature, and write one octave ascending and descending. Check the clef!

Now write a G♭ major scale, one octave descending using accidentals (also in semibreves). Check the clef!

Name these key signatures. The note in each bar is the **mediant** of that key.

_____   _____   _____   _____   _____

Write these key signatures and scale degrees. Watch out for clef changes!

B♭ major   E♭ minor   B♭ minor   C minor
supertonic   leading note   dominant   leading note

Write the tonic (I), subdominant (IV) and dominant (V) triads in root position in our two new keys with six flats in the key signature. Once again, check the clef and be careful with the leading note!

E♭ minor   G♭ major

Here is a melody which features a bunch of flats:

Chopin

What key is it in? (Hint: make a list of all the flats, in key signature order. It's a minor key.) _____

Rewrite the melody here, with a key signature instead of accidentals (don't forget, you may need to include accidentals for a raised 7th degree):

Now write it AGAIN, in the alto clef (with the key signature), sounding one octave lower.

 DID YOU KNOW... our new keys with six sharps/flats are **enharmonic equivalents** of each other. Go and play all the scales you wrote on page 8 followed by the scales you wrote on page 6. They sound exactly the same!

Tenor Clef

In Grade 4, you learned about the alto clef, which looks like this: 𝄡. It is also known as a **C clef**, because it indicates where middle C lies in the stave.

In alto clef, middle C is on the third line: 𝄡 o

Now we're going to learn about another C clef! It is called a **tenor clef**. It looks just like an alto clef, but it is raised up by one line. It's kind of like an alto clef filled with helium!

The tenor clef shows middle C on the fourth line: 𝄡 o   *Wow! This is MIDDLE C! And yes, tenor clef is supposed to stick up above the stave a bit*

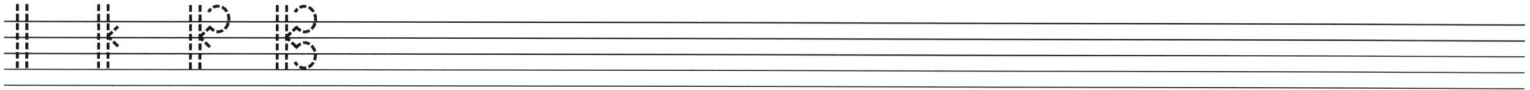

Draw a whole load of tenor clefs here. Make sure they're all centred on the fourth line:

The tenor clef is mostly used by cello, bassoon, and tenor trombone (more about these instruments on pages 47–51) because of the range they often play in. Here is 'Twinkle, Twinkle, Little Star' written in A major, at the same pitch in four different clefs. (Check out the look of the key signatures!) You can see that alto and tenor clefs are easier to read because there are no leger lines. Can you finish off the tune in the other three clefs?

Key signatures look rather different in tenor clef, especially sharp keys:

Write these key signatures in tenor clef:

F# major   Ab major   G# minor   Eb minor   Db major

Rewrite the following notes in tenor clef, keeping the pitch the same. All you need to do is keep the position of middle C (shown in grey) in your head at all times.

Rewrite these short Mozart melodies:

1. In tenor clef, keeping the pitch the same. Remember to write the key signature.

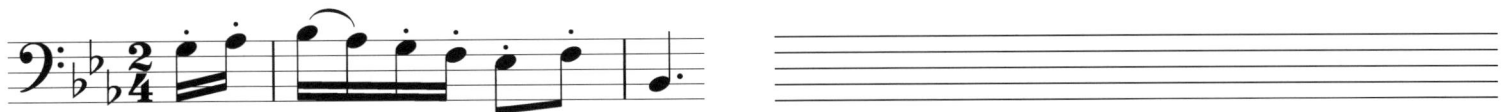

2. In treble clef, sounding one octave **higher**. First, work out the starting note at the same pitch, then put it up an octave!

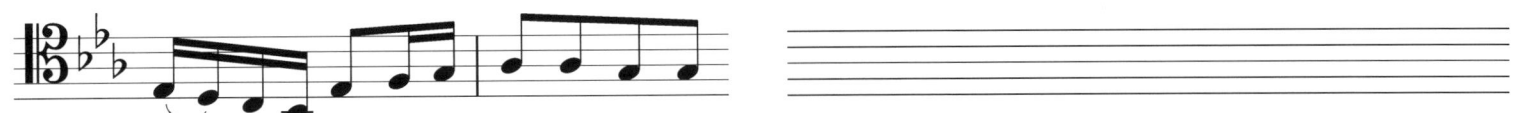

Irregular Time Signatures

In Grade 5 we study four irregular time signatures: $\frac{5}{4}$, $\frac{5}{8}$, $\frac{7}{4}$ and $\frac{7}{8}$. They are irregular because the top number cannot be divided evenly by two or three. This means you'll see a mixture of groups of twos and threes in the same bar!

(The table above shows just a few of the many possible combinations in these time signatures!)

Write the correct time signatures for these one-bar rhythms (and yes, they're all irregular):

Insert the correct time signature AND the missing rests at the places marked *:

Bennett

REMEMBER: these new time signatures are in addition to all the time signatures you learned in Grades 1–4!

The following extracts change time signatures at each place marked with an asterisk.
Insert the correct time signature, choosing from the list below:

$\frac{7}{4}$ $\frac{7}{8}$ $\frac{5}{8}$ $\frac{5}{4}$ $\frac{3}{8}$ $\frac{2}{4}$ $\frac{7}{64}$ $\frac{3}{2}$ $\frac{4}{4}$

DID YOU KNOW... time signatures with a 5 on top are called 'quintuple' time, and time signatures with a 7 on top are called 'septuple' time! Cool, huh?

More Irregular Things

In Grades 3 and 4 you learned about triplets (three notes played in the time of two) and duplets (two notes played in the time of three). Well, there are even more unusual ways to group notes within a beat!

A group of five, six or seven notes, with that number written across the beam, is equal to FOUR notes of that value. Check these out:

Quintuplet:

Sextuplet:

Septuplet:

A run of nine notes is equal to EIGHT of the same value. So:

 HERE'S A THOUGHT: The quintuplets, sextuplets and septuplets above are written as semiquavers, and are equal to one crotchet beat. But if they were grouped with one beam only, i.e. as quavers, each group would be equal to four quavers... which is a minim beat!

Insert the correct time signature for these one-bar rhythms:

14

Not Your Regular Quiz (get it?)

1. Check out this piece by Chopin and answer the questions below.

a) Write the correct number above the irregular group of semiquavers.

b) How many quaver beats would that group be worth? _____

c) What is the key of the piece? _____ (Hint: the right-hand part begins on the mediant)

d) What does 'sostenuto' mean? _____

2. a) Insert the correct time signature for this extract by Bartók:

   b) Name the accents: _____

3. Add the time signature for this piece, also by Bartók (who was clearly very fond of irregular things):

4. How many minims is [9 semiquavers] worth? _____ (Hint: the answer is a fraction)

Compound Intervals

IMPORTANT: Before you go on, make sure you have revised all your Grade 4 interval skills!

Any interval that spans more than one octave is called a **compound** interval. It has the same number and type as if it were one octave smaller, so:

To name any compound interval, simply move the top note down an octave or the bottom note up an octave, then work out the number and type.

Name these intervals, remembering to put the word 'compound' before each:

_____   _____   _____   _____

The other way to name an interval spanning more than an octave is to keep counting the distance between the notes, i.e. instead of 'compound major 2nd' you'd get 'major 9th'. This can really start to add up though, like in this Beethoven melody:

 HOT TIP: No matter which naming system you choose, it's ALWAYS easiest to first rewrite the interval so that both notes are within an octave, before you try to figure out the number and type.

Complete the table on the next page (which uses a technique we learned in Grade 4) for great practice in naming compound intervals!

'Dressed' compound interval	Draw it within an octave and without accidentals ('undress' it)	Name the 'naked' interval	Describe how the accidentals affect the interval	Now name the original interval!
(bass clef: ♯o top, ♭o bottom)	(bass clef: o, o)	minor 2nd	top note is one semitone higher, bottom note is one semitone lower, therefore the interval is two semitones larger	compound augmented 2nd
(treble clef: o top, ♯o bottom)	(treble clef: o, o)			
(bass clef: ♭o top, o bottom)				
(treble clef: ♭o top, ♭o bottom)				
(bass clef: 𝄪o top, ♯o bottom)				

Don't forget: if you need to identify intervals from a piece with a key signature, you'll need to rewrite the interval with accidentals first. For example, simply convert (bass clef with key sig) into (bass clef with accidentals), then work out the name of the interval using the process above!

Describe fully the intervals (by number and type) marked with brackets in this melody:

Liszt

_____   _____   _____

17

Intervals and Things

Name the intervals marked A, B and C with brackets. Remember, it's easiest to rewrite compound intervals within an octave, and with accidentals instead of a key signature, to work out the number and type. If you need spare manuscript go to **www.blitzbooks.com**.

Interval A _____ Interval B _____ Interval C _____

Interval A _____ Interval B _____ Interval C _____

Interval A _____ Interval B _____ Interval C _____

Interval A _____ Interval B _____ Interval C _____

On this page you have to name the intervals AND insert the missing time signature for each example! There are also some Bonus Things To Do (after all, this isn't called Intervals and Things for nothing).

Saint-Saëns

Interval A _____   Interval B _____   Interval C _____

Bonus Thing To Do: Add the missing triplet signs in bar 2.

Rimsky-Korsakov

Interval A _____   Interval B _____   Interval C _____

Bonus Thing To Do: True or False: The first tied note is equal to a dotted crotchet. _____

Fauré

Interval A _____   Interval B _____   Interval C _____

Bonus Things To Do: Is the time signature simple or compound? _____

   Is it duple, triple or quadruple? _____

What does 'espress.' mean? _____

Let's Test Your Skills So Far

Here are two pieces of music and a whole load of questions to answer on each. You'll need to use all of the skills you've learned so far in this book (plus ALL the skills you learned in Grades 1-4, of course!).

Mussorgsky

★ Name the two possible keys of the extract above: _____ and _____

★ Insert time signatures at the places marked *

★ Rewrite the first two bars an octave lower, using the tenor clef. Remember to include the key signature.

★ Write as a breve the enharmonic equivalent of the third note in bar 1.

★ True or false: the left-hand part consists entirely of octaves. _____

★ Name and explain the signs on the notes in bars 1 and 2: _____

★ Who wrote this music? _____ (not difficult, if you're observant)

★ Fully describe the interval marked with the letter Y in bar 4: _____

Chopin

★ The key of this piece is ____ minor. Write one octave ascending of that harmonic minor scale here, using the treble clef and semibreves. Use accidentals instead of a key signature.

★ What is the relative major key of the scale you just wrote? _____

★ Write as a breve the enharmonic equivalent of the note marked *.

★ Insert the correct time signature (hint: it's compound time)

Watch out! Key signature here!

★ Name the ornament in bar 3: _____

★ Ignoring that ornament, rewrite bars 2 and 3 of the treble melody, using notes of HALF the value. Write the key signature, the new time signature, and make sure you group the notes correctly.

★ What does 'cantabile' mean? _____

★ Fully describe the intervals marked with brackets under the bass stave. (Be careful! They are VERY tricky, because of the key signature! You may want to rewrite them with accidentals, on spare manscript.)

Interval A _____   Interval B _____   Interval C _____

Transposing Instruments

Most instruments of the orchestra are non-transposing, which means they sound at **concert pitch**. For example, when flutes play a C, it actually comes out sounding like a C. This means:

Flute music that looks like this sounds like this

You may be thinking, 'that's SO obvious, why are we even discussing this?'! Well, it's because not all instruments behave like that! Some instruments are **transposing instruments**.

INSTRUMENTS IN B FLAT (e.g. clarinet in B flat, trumpet)

When these guys play a C, they get the sound of... B flat! This is why they are called 'instruments in B flat' (and it's due to the convoluted evolution of these instruments, which we won't go into right now). So:

Trumpet music that looks like this sounds like this

★ Instruments in B flat sound a major 2nd (__ semitones) lower than written. ★

INSTRUMENTS IN A (e.g. clarinet in A, cornet in A)

When these guys play a C, the get the sound of... A! So, for instruments in A:

Music that looks like this sounds like this

★ Instruments in A sound a minor 3rd (__ semitones) lower than written. ★

And finally...

INSTRUMENTS IN F (e.g. horn, cor anglais)

When these guys play a C, they get the sound of... you guessed it... an F! So:

Horn music that looks like this sounds like this

★ Instruments in F sound a perfect 5th (__ semitones) lower than written. ★

The way music is written for transposing instruments is called **written pitch**. The way it sounds is called **concert pitch**. Can you fill in the rest of the concert pitch notes?

	Written pitch (i.e. what they play)	Will actually sound	**Concert pitch** (i.e. what we hear)
Instruments in B flat	(music notation)	Down a major 2nd	(music notation)
Instruments in A	(music notation)	Down a minor 3rd	(music notation)
Instruments in F	(music notation)	Down a perfect 5th	(music notation)

HOT TIP: When transposing from concert pitch to written pitch, all the notes will go UP a major 2nd / minor 3rd / perfect 5th!

Some instruments are called transposing instruments but do not actually change key. They simply sound an octave higher/lower than written. For example:

Piccolos sound an octave **higher** than written. (Can you fill in the sounding pitch?)

Their music looks like but sounds like

some serious leger lines needed here

Double basses sound an octave **lower** than written.

Their music looks like but sounds like

Did you know, there are quite a few more transposing instruments than are listed here? Can you research and list three? _____, _____ and _____.

More about Transposing

When transposing from written pitch to concert pitch and vice versa, the rhythm and shape of the transposed melody must be the same as the original. However, lots of the time the accidentals will CHANGE! (Veeeery tricky)

For example, here is a melody in C major. In bar 2, you'll see it has a sharp which is straight away cancelled by a natural:

If we wanted a clarinet in B flat to make the sound of the melody above, we have to transpose it **up a major 2nd**, to D major. You'll notice that the accidentals remain the same (fill in the missing notes, which should all be two semitones higher than the original):

But what if the C major melody WAS the written pitch? To get concert pitch, we would have to transpose it **down a tone**, to B flat major (fill in the missing notes, all a tone lower). As you can see, in this version the accidentals CHANGE:

The most important thing to remember is that accidentals do a job:

A sharp sign (♯) always **raises** a note by one semitone

A flat sign (♭) always **lowers** a note by one semitone

A natural sign (♮) could be raising **or** lowering a note – it depends on the key signature – or it could be cancelling out a sharp or a flat!

Adjusting Accidentals

Each of the following melodies has been transposed for you (hooray!) except for the accidentals (boo). Work out what 'job' each accidental is doing: write 'R' for raised and 'L' for lowered on each one. Then add the correct accidentals to the transposed melodies!

Careful! Look at the key signature!

  HOT TIP: when transposing a perfect 5th up or down, remember that B to F is not a perfect 5th! B up a perfect 5th is F#, and F down a perfect 5th is B♭.

Transpose these yourself! First, label the accidentals, then write the new notes, then adjust the accidentals where necessary.

25

Transposing Tricks

Here is a cool trick to help you find the new notes in your transposed melody. You can write a table that shows you how each note changes. For example, if your original melody has two sharps in the key signature, write the letter names of the MAJOR scale with two sharps:

| Original key: **D major** | D | E | F# | G | A | B | C# | D |

Let's say you have to transpose it up a minor 3rd. Find the MAJOR scale of the note a minor 3rd (three semitones) higher: F major! Write these letter names directly below the D major letter names.

| Original key: **D major** | D | E | F# | G | A | B | C# | D |
| Up minor 3rd: **F major** | F | G | A | B♭ | C | D | E | F |

Now you can see that D will become F; E will become G; F# will become A (not A#!), etc.

Let's test this out with a melody in D major, so that we can use the table above. First, label all the accidentals with 'R' or 'L', just like we did on the previous page:

Now transpose the melody up a minor 3rd (to be written for, say, cornet in A). Write the new key signature, and move all the notes. Remember to use the table above to help! (Remember that you won't actually need to write a flat sign next to the Bs in your transposed melody, because you'll have a key signature.)

Now copy 'R' and 'L' in all the same spots, and adjust all the accidentals according to those labels. (Be careful when raising the Bs — you'll need a natural!) Yay, your melody is transposed!

HOT TIP: If you're transposing using key signatures, you can actually write your transposing table without any sharps/flats against the letter names. You'll still need to label and adjust all the accidentals!

You can use transposing tables in any situation. If the given melody has no key signature, simply assume it's C major! Let's try it with this melody by Brahms. Transpose it up a perfect 5th, as it would be written for horn. (But first, label the accidentals, of course!)

Original key: **C major**	C	D	E	F	G	A	B	C
Up perfect 5th: **G major**	G							

Now write the new key signature and transpose the melody. (And, of course, remember to add the 'R' and 'L' labels and adjust the accidentals.)

Occasionally the exam question can be a bit tricky. You're given a melody with a key signature, and asked to transpose it WITHOUT using a key signature! Just write your table very carefully, including all sharps/flats in the new scale, and follow it to the letter (ha ha).

This is the cor anglais part from music by Bizet. Write it as it would sound at concert pitch.

Assume the key is major

Original key: _____	
Down perfect 5th: _____	

Include all the accidentals shown in the table, THEN make the adjustments.

That's it! You're now a transposition expert!

Let's Transpose

1. These are the actual sounds made by a horn in F. Transpose this to its written pitch, i.e. up a perfect 5th. Write the new key signature.

    Chopin

2. This melody is in written for clarinet in A. Write the melody in concert pitch, i.e. down a minor 3rd, without a key signature.

    Tchaikovsky

3. Here is another melody by Tchaikovsky, written at concert pitch. Rewrite it for clarinet in B flat, i.e. up a major 2nd. Write the new key signature.

A Bit of Revision

1. Write the scale of D# melodic minor:

    ★ use a key signature
    ★ use crotchets
    ★ write one octave ascending and then descending

2. Transpose this melody so that it is at written pitch for cornet in A (so, up a minor 3rd).

3. Write the following key signatures and the named scale degree for each.

| F# major | A minor | D♭ major | C# minor | E♭ minor |
| submediant | leading note | subdominant | dominant | leading note |

4. Fill each of these bars with **one sound**. (Hint: you may need to use tied notes in some of them!)

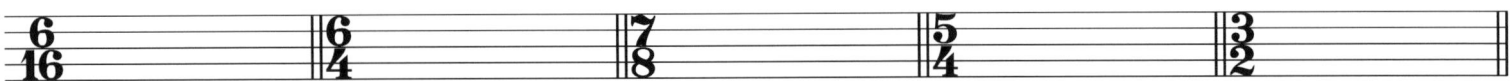

Chord II

In Grade 4 we studied the three primary triads: chords I, IV and V. Now we're going to add chord II! It's the SUPERTONIC chord, which of course is built on scale degree no. 2.

> N.B. We always use Roman numerals when referring to chord numbers. For now, the numerals are always upper case. In higher grades, you'll learn about lower-case numerals.

Each of these chords is the supertonic triad of its key. Name each key.

Key: _____   _____   _____   _____   _____

Label each chord marked with an asterisk below as I, II, IV or V. They are all in root position, so you really only need to look at the bottom note of each chord!

Your hint for identifying the key: the piece ends on the tonic chord.

Welsh ballad tune

Write chord II in root position in the named keys. Use accidentals. Watch out for clef changes!

C minor   A major   G major   F minor   F♯ minor

First and Second Inversion

Up until now we've only dealt with triads in root position, i.e. the root of the chord is the bottom note, and the 3rd and 5th of the chord sit above it.

Here's the thing – if we change the order of the notes, we get two different **inversions**:

First inversion means that the **3rd** of the chord is the bottom note

Second inversion means that the **5th** of the chord is the bottom note

There are two shortcuts for naming the position of any chord. The first is to use the letters a (root position), b (first inversion) and c (second inversion) after the Roman numeral. So, if you are referring to chord IV in second inversion, you can just call it IVc!

The other shortcut is to use **figures**. Root position is called $\frac{5}{3}$, first inversion is called $\frac{6}{3}$ and second inversion is called $\frac{6}{4}$. These figures refer to the intervals above the bass note:

Root position ($\frac{5}{3}$)   First inversion ($\frac{6}{3}$)   Second inversion ($\frac{6}{4}$)

3 ways to name chords!	Words	Letters	Figures
Root	Root position	a (e.g. Ia)	$\frac{5}{3}$ (e.g. I^5_3)
3rd	_____ inversion	b (e.g. Ib)	$\frac{6}{3}$ (e.g. I^6_3)
5th	_____ inversion	c (e.g. Ic)	$\frac{6}{4}$ (e.g. I^6_4)

More on Chord Positions

The bottom note of ANY chord tells you its position, no matter what order the other notes are in! Here is the tonic chord of G major, in various positions. Write the letters a, b or c next to each Roman numeral to show the position. (The first one is done for you, yay)

Chord I of G major consists of the notes G, B and D in any order.

B is the bottom note here, which means this chord is in first inversion!

Ib   I_   I_   I_   I_   I_

Let's do that again, this time using figures! These chords are all chord IV of A major.

Chord IV of A major contains D, F and A (and sometimes the A might be missing).

The bottom note is the one that tells you the position of the chord.

IV$_3^5$ IV☐   IV☐   IV☐   IV☐   IV☐

Here is a chord progression in B♭ major, with chord numbers underneath (and the notes of that chord written above, just to help out a bit). Can you label the position of each chord? You can use letters OR figures – choose a method and stick to it!

(BDF) (FAC)   (EGB)   (CEG)

I   V   I   IV   II   I   I   V

The positions of the last two chords in the example above form a really important chord progression in music. Chord I in second inversion followed by chord V in root position is often referred to without Roman numerals and is known as the $_4^6$ $_3^5$ progression. It always occurs on the dominant note of the key. More about this later!

Identifying Chords

There is a super easy way to identify any chord and its position. All you need to do is draw a little grid containing the letter names of chords I, II, IV and V (in root position order) in any particular key. For example, complete this C major grid:

Things to Notice

Key: C major			
I	C	E	G
II	D	F	A
IV	F	A	_
V	G	_	_
	a	b	c

This shows the position of the chord. It's much easier to call the columns a, b and c, rather than using figures!

★ There are three columns of letter names

★ Column a shows the **root** of each chord.

★ Column b shows the **3rd** of each chord.

★ Column c shows the **5th** of each chord.

So, this grid is going to help us identify the chord **number** by matching up the letter names, and the chord **position** by checking whether the bass note comes from column a, b or c!

Let's identify this chord. The key is D minor, so first we have to write a D minor grid!

1. List the notes you see in the chord. Ignore repeated notes. _____

2. Which chord number in the grid contains those notes? ____

3. Does the **bottom note** of the chord come from column a, b, or c? ____ That means this chord is in root position / first inversion / second inversion (circle correct answer)

4. So the final answer is: _____. Easy! (IIb? Or not IIb? That IS the question. Ha. Ha ha. Ha ha ha ha.)

HOT TIP: You'll get used to reading your grids quickly the more you practise. The rows tell you the chords and the columns tell you the positions! Write out grids in lots of different keys.

Let's I.D. Chords

In case it's not completely obvious from the title of this page, identify each chord marked with an asterisk, naming the chord number and its position. You can choose to use letters or figures to name the position (hooray).

To make it easy, complete a chord grid in the key of each new extract below (they are all major keys, hooray again).

All of the extracts contain the $^6_4$ $^5_3$ (Ic – Va) progression we talked about earlier. Put a circle around these two chords when you find them!

Key:

I			
II			
IV			
V			
	a	b	c

Traditional

Traditional

Rowlands

SATB: Vocal Ranges

The letters SATB stand for the four voices in a choir – soprano, alto, tenor and bass.

The highest voice is called SOPRANO
The second-highest voice is called ALTO
⟵ These are usually female voices

The second-lowest voice is called TENOR
The lowest voice is called BASS
⟵ These are usually male voices

Here are the typical ranges used in vocal music:

In real life many singers can reach notes well outside these ranges! However, you can be sure that if you stick to these ranges when writing for voice you won't put anyone outside their comfort zone.

Sing some songs with your teacher. Which vocal range is best for you? _____

DID YOU KNOW... Female voices with a range in between soprano and alto are called 'mezzo-soprano'. Male voices with a range in between tenor and bass are called 'baritone'. Interesting, huh?

Name the type of voice that best suits these melodies, given the range of notes:

Short Test

1. This music adapted from Schubert is in the key of ___ major. Label the chords marked with an asterisk.

2. Now rewrite the soprano (top) part up a minor 3rd.

3. What is the name for the vocal range between soprano and alto? _____

4. What is the name for the vocal range between tenor and bass? _____

5. Study this excerpt by Dvořák and answer the questions below.

   a) What does lento mean? _____ What does ♪ = 112 refer to? _____

   b) There is an irregular time division in this melody. Find it and write the correct number underneath.

   c) Name two ornaments in this extract. _____

   d) Look ahead to the instrument ranges on pages 47-51. Name three instruments that could play this piece: _____

Awesome work!

RESULT: BLITZED IT / PASSED / TRY AGAIN (circle correct answer)

Another Short Test (lucky you)

As usual, answer questions about this music.

Monti

1. Which two instruments is this music mostly likely written for? _____ and piano.

2. Ignoring the ornaments, rewrite the solo part from the beginning until the end of bar 2 in the **treble** clef, sounding one octave higher. Write the key signature.

3. They key is G minor. Bar 1 of the piano part consists of chord I. Which inversion is played in the right hand? _____

4. Working from your answer to question 2 above, transpose it down a major 2nd, as it would sound if played by a clarinet in B flat. Write the new key signature.

5. Find and circle the $^6_4{}^5_3$ (Ic - Va) chord progression in this traditional music.

RESULT: BLITZED IT / PASSED / TRY AGAIN (circle correct answer)

Cadences

A cadence consists of two chords that finish off a musical phrase. On the next page we'll be talking about cadences in melodies. In Grade 5 we study three types of cadence. Here's an example of each, in C major:

PERFECT CADENCE

The **perfect cadence** consists of chords **V – I**. It is like a musical full stop. A LOT of pieces end with a perfect cadence!

IMPERFECT CADENCE

The **imperfect cadence** consists of **any chord leading to chord V**. Since chord V sounds very unfinished, the imperfect cadence is like a question mark in music. (II–V shown here, but I–V and IV–V are also imperfect cadences!)

PLAGAL CADENCE

The **plagal cadence** consists of chords **IV – I**. It is very common to hear this at the end of a hymn (the 'amen' bit), after the perfect cadence. Think of a plagal cadence as a few words in brackets after you've made your final point.

Complete this table:

NAME OF CADENCE	CHORDS USED	DESCRIBE IN PUNCTUATION TERMS
	V – I	
Imperfect		
		An extra comment after final point

DID YOU KNOW... There is a fourth type of cadence, called an 'interrupted cadence'. It consists of chords V–VI. This cadence is like a musical semicolon! You'll be learning more about this cadence in higher grades.

More About Cadences

Can you identify the perfect, plagal and imperfect cadences in this music by Purcell? The key is.... well, you can work out the key. (Go back to page 38 to check out which chords make up which cadences)

Cadence X:_____   Cadence Y:_____ Cadence Z:_____

Good work! In your exam it's a little different... rather than actually naming or identifying cadences, you have to choose which chords will sound best under certain melody notes. For example, you'll get a melody with sets of bracketed notes, like this:

Step 1: Identify the key of the melody (C, G, F, or D major): _____

Step 2: On some spare paper, write a chord grid in that key.

Step 3: Find the chord that contains the majority of the notes under each bracket - it will always be either I, II, IV or V.

Once you've decided on which chords will fit, write I, II, IV or V in the boxes underneath the stave. (Make sure you only use one chord per box!)

39

Good work! Now you can use exactly the same strategy to work out the best chords in the following melodies.

 HERE'S A THOUGHT... In a group of three chords, the first of the three chords is called the **approach chord** and the next two chords form the actual cadence.

Sometimes more than one chord will suit the note or notes under each bracket. You have to make a decision which is best, and this is where your knowledge of cadences really kicks in!

★ Remember there is no such thing as a cadence that ends on II or IV.

★ If you have a choice between chords II and IV, it's a safe choice to go with chord IV. Remember there is no such cadence as II – I!

Practice Makes Perfect (and imperfect and plagal ha ha)

For each of these, identify the key and use chord grids to help you decide on the chords.

Ornaments

In Grade 4 you had to recognise and name ornaments. In Grade 5 you also need the skill of replacing the actual sound with the correct ornament!

Actual Sound	Replace with	Name of Ornament
		Upper mordent (no vertical line) / Lower mordent (with vertical line)
		Trill (or 'shake')
		Acciaccatura or 'crushed note' (little line through tail)
		Appoggiatura or 'leaning note' (no line through tail)
		Turn
		Turn (between notes)
		Arpeggiation (or 'fanning' of the notes)

Other things to know:

★ Ornaments may have accidentals, e.g. 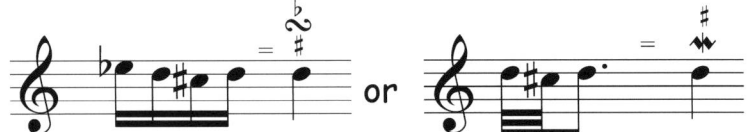 or

★ When you draw a turn, think of it as a backwards 'S' lying on its side! ∽

★ Two or more grace notes look like this: . They can be played as acciaccaturas (crushed notes) or appoggiaturas (leaning notes), depending on the style of music!

Repetitions and Repeats

Composers use shortcuts when notes, bars, phrases and sections of music are repeated. You already know quite a few of these, like the repeat dots at a double bar, 'D.C. al fine', the 'dal segno' sign (𝄋), that sort of thing. But here are a few you may not have seen before!

Written	Played	Written	Played
(whole note)	(repeated notes)	(note with tremolo)	(repeated notes)
(half note)	(repeated notes)	(note with tremolo)	(repeated notes)
(quarter note)	(repeated notes)	(note with tremolo)	(repeated notes)
(quarter note)	(repeated notes)	(bass clef note with slash)	(repeated notes)

There are even repeat signs for whole bars of music:

Repeat the previous bar

Repeat the previous two bars

Let's test your skills. Check out this music by Wagner:

★ Write a sign here that could replace all the notes in bar 2. _____

★ Write bar 1 as it would sound: _____

★ True or false: This entire melody is to be repeated. _____

Quick Quiz

Andante religioso — Massenet

1. Add an ornament to make this bar sound the same as bar 3.

2. Draw a sign in bar 2 of the bass stave to show that it is a repeat of bar 1.

3. How many demisemiquavers is the quintuplet in bar 3 worth? ___

4. What does 'andante religioso' mean? _____
   ('Religioso' is not on your list of terms, but you could have a good pretty good guess)

5. Rewrite the treble melody one octave lower, using the alto clef.

6. What is the currency of New Zealand? _____ (not essential Grade 5 knowledge)

7. Rewrite the following music by Scarlatti with correct grouping/beaming of notes and rests (it's been a while since you've been tested on this, lucky you).

Terms

Notice how this page is not called '**Italian** Terms'? That's because there are some GERMAN terms to learn in Grade 5 as well as Italian! (Lucky you) Remember, you need to know these **in addition to** all the terms you learned in Grades 1–4. Find them all at **www.blitzbooks.com**, and you can also check out **How to Blitz! Musical Knowledge.**

Italian

attacca	-	go on at once
dolente	-	mournful, sad
dolore, doloroso	-	grief, sorrowful
doppio movimento	-	twice as fast
estinto	-	lifeless
incalzando	-	getting quicker
lacrimoso	-	sad
loco	-	at normal pitch
lunga	-	long (e.g. for a pause)
lusingando	-	in a persuasive style
misura	-	measure
ossia	-	or, alternative
piacevole	-	pleasant
piangevole	-	plaintive
pochettino (poch.)	-	rather little
rinforzando (rf, rfz)	-	reinforced sound
smorzando (smorz.)	-	dying away (volume and tempo)
teneramente	-	tenderly
tenerezza	-	tenderness
tosto	-	swift
volante	-	flying (fast)

German

aber	-	but
bewegt	-	with quick movement, agitated
breit	-	broad
ein	-	one
einfach	-	simple
etwas	-	somewhat
fröhlich	-	cheerful, joyful
immer	-	always
langsam	-	slow
lebhaft	-	lively
mässig	-	at a moderate speed
mit Ausdruck	-	with expression
nicht	-	not
ohne	-	without
ruhig	-	calm, peaceful
schnell	-	fast
sehr	-	very
süss	-	sweet
traurig	-	sad
und	-	and
voll	-	full
wenig	-	little
wieder	-	again
zart	-	tender, delicate
zu	-	too

Tiny Test

1. Translate these German instructions:

   mit Ausdruck aber nicht zu schnell _____

   langsam und immer sehr ruhig _____

2. Here is some music by Chopin, followed by (surprise, surprise) some exercises relating to it:

   ★ What key is it in? The last note is the mediant. _____

   ★ What does '*rfz*' stand for and what does it mean? _____

   ★ What does '*teneramente*' mean? _____

   ★ The quintuplet in bar 3 is the written form of which ornament? _____

   ★ Add an ornament to this chord which would make it sound the same as the circled notes in bars 3-4.

   ★ Add a sign to show that the last chord in the left hand should be arpeggiated.

   ★ Add an Italian term to show that the last treble note should be played at normal pitch.

3. Fill in this table with matching terms in each of three languages (wow, you're multilingual now!):

FRENCH	GERMAN	ITALIAN
cédez		*ritardando*
	langsam	
		meno
	ruhig	
très		

The String Family

Instrument	Approximate Range	Common Terms and Signs	Interesting Facts About Strings
Violin		*con sordino*: play with mute *sul ponticello*: play on or near the bridge ∨ up bow ⊓ down bow *arco*: with the bow *pizzicato*: pluck the strings *sul G*: play on the G string double-stopping: playing two or more notes at once	★ The bow is drawn across the strings to make them vibrate and produce sound ★ Double bass music is written an octave higher than it sounds ★ The full name for cello is actually 'violoncello' ★ A slur over the notes indicates to play in one bow ★ The open strings of the violin, viola and cello are all a 5th apart ★ The open strings of a double bass are a 4th apart
Viola			
Cello			
Double Bass			

Insert the correct sign where indicated:

i) down bow

ii) lower mordent

iii) up bow

iv) a direction to pluck the strings

v) a direction to play with the bow

47

The Woodwind Family

Instrument	Approximate Written Range	Common Terms and Signs	Interesting Facts About Woodwinds
Piccolo		Flutter tonguing	★ Air is blown across or into the mouthpiece or reed to make the column of air vibrate.
Flute		, (breath mark)	★ The piccolo sounds an octave higher than written.
Oboe			★ Flute and piccolo are the only non-reed instruments.
Clarinet			★ The oboe, cor anglais and bassoon are double-reed instruments.
Bass Clarinet			★ The clarinet is a single-reed instrument.
Cor Anglais			★ The bass clarinet sounds one octave lower than the B♭ clarinet.
Bassoon			★ All clarinets are notated within the same written range, and all in treble clef.
Contrabassoon (or double bassoon)			★ The bassoon and contrabassoon often use tenor clef.

★ The contrabassoon sounds one octave lower than written.

★ The saxophone is another single-reed woodwind instrument but is not usually in an orchestra.

The Brass Family

Instrument	Approximate Written Range	Interesting Facts About Brass	Common Terms and Signs
Trumpet		★ The brass section use mutes, but they are very different to string mutes. They are conical objects that are inserted into the bell of the instrument.	*con sordino*: play with mute *fp* (forte-piano): loud then immediately soft
Horn		★ The horn is the only brass instrument included in a wind quintet (along with flute, oboe, clarinet and bassoon). ★ The horn, trombone and tuba are also known as the French horn, tenor trombone and bass tuba.	
Trombone		Tuba	

Here is the theme from Mozart's famous horn concerto. Answer the questions below:

senza sordino

★ What does *senza sordino* mean? _____

★ Bar 5 is a repeat of bar 1. Write it as it will sound.

The Percussion Family

UNPITCHED PERCUSSION		
Instrument	Common Terms and Signs	Interesting Facts About Percussion
Cymbals	Roll (like a trill) ✗ (unpitched notehead)	★ Most percussion instruments are struck with sticks or mallets (or against each other, as with cymbals). ★ Other unpitched percussion instruments also found in the orchestra include castanets and bongo drums.
Side drum		
Bass drum		
Triangle		

PITCHED PERCUSSION		
Instrument	Common Terms and Signs	Interesting Facts About Percussion
Timpani	Roll (like a trill)	★ Other pitched percussion instruments also found in the orchestra include tubular bells and chime bars.
Xylophone		
Glockenspiel		
Marimba		

The Keyboard Family

Instrument	Common Terms and Signs	Interesting Facts About Keyboard Instruments
Piano	*una corda (u.c.)* ('one string'): depress the soft pedal *tre corde (t.c.)* ('three strings'): release the soft pedal *m.s/m.d*: 'left hand'/'right hand' (Italian) *m.g/m.d*: 'left hand'/'right hand' (French)	★ The first pianos were made in Italy in the early 1700s. Using hammers to strike the strings, they gave performers close control over a wide range of dynamics. Upright pianos came along around 100 years later. ★ Modern pianos usually have 88 keys, giving just over seven octaves. Most have at least two pedals – a 'soft' pedal and a 'sustain' pedal – and some might have a 'sostenuto' pedal, which allows the performer to choose which notes to sustain, or a very quiet 'practice' pedal.
Organ		
Harpsichord	Harp*	Celesta

*Harp is not really a keyboard instrument but it has a range similar to piano. It is an orchestral instrument most often associated with the strings section.

Here is some piano music by Moszkowski that features many of the signs listed above. Discuss each one of these with your teacher!

Crossword

Wow, you have certainly learned a lot in this book, especially in the last few pages! It's time to put your knowledge to the test (but not a very serious test). Complete the crossword below by solving the 'across' and 'down' clues. Have fun!

Across

1. Term for bowing two strings at once
9. Piccolo music sounds this much higher than written
11. Clef often used by cello and bassoon
13. G♯ is the _____ equivalent of A♭
14. Music for B flat instruments must be transposed ___ __ _____ (2, 1, 4)
17. Italian term for 'alternative part'
19. Word that applies both to volume in music and properties in physics

20. Interval spanning more than an octave
25. The strings of a bow are actually made of these, from a horse's tail
26. Highest female voice
28. Name of 'The Magic Dragon'
29. G, D, A and E are the _____ strings on a violin.
30. Number and type of this interval:
33. Something no teenager can do without
35. Family of instruments to which the celesta belongs
36. Unlike the rest of the string family, the double bass is tuned in _____
37. Very low bassoon
38. German term for 'little'

Down

2. G, D, A and E are the _____ string tunings of the violin
3. English meaning of 'breit'
4. You must do this to written music for clarinet otherwise it will sound wrong with piano
5. Non-transposing instruments sound at concert _____
6. In Grade 5 you need to know Italian, French and _____ terms
7. Type of this 6th:
8. Italian term for 'go straight on'
10. Alto clef and tenor clef are both also known as a _____
12. Brass instrument that sometimes uses tenor clef
15. The clarinet in A sounds this much lower than written
16. Male voice in between bass and tenor
18. Relative of the oboe
21. Type of scale with a raised 6th and 7th ascending
22. Time signatures with 5, 7 or 8 as the top number are known as this
23. These are used to raise the leading notes in G♯ and D♯ minor
24. Scale degree no. 2
26. $\frac{6}{4}$ chords are in this inversion
27. Key with six flats (doesn't matter whether you pick major or minor)
31. German term for 'at a moderate speed'
32. Lower type of soprano voice/Italian for 'medium'
34. Italian abbreviation for 'held back'

Use Your Skills

It's time to answer more questions about lots of different excerpts of music. Have fun!

Fauré

★ Insert the missing time signature.

★ Name and explain the squiggly line on the first chord of the piano part:
_____

★ Why is the solo part in a different key from the piano part? _____
_____

★ The key is E♭ major. Name the chord number and inversion of the circled chord in bar 9: _____

★ Give the English meaning of the following terms:

rf _____

volante _____

Tosto _____

★ Name the ornament in bar 4: _____

★ Rewrite bar 2, replacing the first two notes with an ornament:

★ Insert the time signature.

★ Bar 7 should sound like this: Add the missing ornament above.

★ What is the value of the last note of bar 1? _____

★ Fully describe the interval marked X: _____

★ Put a bracket over four consecutive notes that form a chromatic scale.

★ Explain the signs |1. |2. _____

★ For how many beats will the last chord sound? _____

★ How many different types of repeat signs are in this extract? _____

★ Name two instruments that could play this music: _____

★ Add an Italian term to show that the second bar should be played twice as fast.

★ Rewrite the last chord of the right hand in the tenor clef:

55

Fauré

★ Name two keys that share the key signature of this piece: _____

★ How many double flats are in this excerpt? ____

★ Explain the tempo marking: _____

★ Explain 'm.d.' (bar 2): _____

★ Explain how the last five semiquavers in bar 3 are to be played: _____
_____

★ Rewrite the circled chord in bar 4 enharmonically, without accidentals:

★ True or false: Hermione Granger's parents were dentists. _____

★ There is a change of time signature in bar 6. Insert the correct one.

★ Insert the missing rest/s at the place marked with an asterisk in bar 6.

★ This music is written for a solo transposing woodwind instrument with piano accompaniment. Name the solo instrument: _____

★ Which bars contain irregular subdivisions? _____

★ How many semiquavers is the circled note in bar 6 worth? _____

★ How many bars feature demisemiquavers? _____

★ Rewrite bar 4 (solo part) at concert pitch:

★ How many times does the tonic chord feature in the piano part? (It's in a major key) _____

★ Explain the tempo marking: _____

Test Paper... Sort Of

All theory books end with a test paper, but this one is DIFFERENT. It already has the answers in it (mostly wrong answers!) and your job is to be the teacher – you have to **mark** it.

When you've found all the mistakes, go to **www.blitzbooks.com** and download the EXACT SAME PAPER – this time with no answers already in it. See if you can get 100%!

★ ★ ★ ★ ★ ★ ★

Theory Paper Grade 5
Time allowed: 2 hours

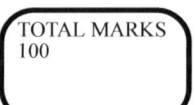

1 a) The following extract begins on the first beat of the bar. Put in the missing bar-lines.

(3)

b) Look at the following extract by Albéniz and then answer the questions below.

i) Describe the chords marked A and B as I, II, IV or V. Also indicate whether the lowest note of the chord is the root (a), 3rd (b) or 5th (c). The key is E major.

Chord **A** .... Ia .... (2)

Chord **B** .... 5a .... (2)

ii) Insert the correct time signature. (2)

iii) Name two keys that share the key signature of this extract

...E maj... and ...C min... (2)

iv) True or false: the last bar contains the sound of a G natural. ...False... (1)

v) Rewrite the first chord of the left-hand (bass) part in the tenor clef at the same pitch. Remember to write the key signature. (3)

2 Describe fully (e.g. major 2nd) each of these melodic intervals.

...major 4th...

...compound min 3rd...

...perfect 4th...

...major 7th...

...minor 2nd...

3 The following melody is written for clarinet in B flat. Transpose it down a major 2nd, as will sound at concert pitch. Do not use a key signature, but add all necessary accidentals.

Leoncavallo

59

4 Study this music by Schumann and answer the questions that follow. (30)

i) This music is written for one stringed instrument and one keyboard instrument. (2)
Name the two most likely. ......Piano........ and ....viola..........

ii) Name three different ornaments in this piece, stating the bar in which each occurs. (6)

Ornament ....trill........ Ornament ....trill........ Ornament ....mordent........
Bar ....4........ Bar ....5........ Bar ....7........

iii) Rewrite the circled chord in bar 3 so that it sounds at the same pitch, but using the tenor C clef. Remember to write the clef and the key signature. (4)

iv) Explain the 𝓟𝓮𝓭.⎦ sign under bar 5. ...Ped = foot, so use your foot... (2)

v) Describe the chords marked X and Y in bar 4 as I, II, IV or V in the key of F major. Also indicate whether the lowest note of the chord is the root (a), 3rd (b) or 5th (c). (4)

X ......Ia......

Y ......IVa......

vi) Give the English meaning of: (6)

Mit Ausdruck ......with feeling......

fp (bar 1) ......loud and soft at the same time......

cresc. (bar 4) ......crescendo......

vii) Give the name of the voice part that lies between soprano and alto in vocal range. (2)

......Sopralto......

viii) Underline one instrument below that is a member of the orchestral brass family. (2)

oboe   <u>french horn</u>   tambourine   celesta

ix) Name two instruments from the woodwind family that use bass clef. (2)

......Bassoon and bass clarinet......

61

5 a) Write the key signature of five sharps and then one octave descending of the melodic minor scale with that key signature.

b) Place accidentals in front of any necessary notes in order to form a G♭ chromatic scale. Do not use a key signature.

6 Look at the extract and then answer the questions below.

 etc.

a) Tick one box. (1)

$\frac{12}{8}$ signifies:

compound quadruple ✓

simple quadruple ☐

compound triple ☐

simple triple ☐

b) (i) Give the technical name (e.g. tonic, dominant) of the note marked X. Remember that the key is E♭ major.

..........tonic.......... (2)

(ii) Write as a breve (double whole-note) an enharmonic equivalent of the note marked Y. (2)

(iii) Rewrite bar 1 in simple time but without changing the rhythmic effect. Remember to put in the key signature and the new time signature. (4)

c) (i) Answer TRUE or FALSE to the following statement:

The cello is a transposing instrument................FALSE............... (2)

(ii) The cello is a member of the string family of orchestral instruments. Name a standard orchestral instrument from a different family that could play this extract so that it sounds at the same pitch, and state the family of instruments to which it belongs.

Instrument ......bassoon............ Family ....reed............... (4)

7 Suggest chord progressions for two cadences in the following melody by writing I, II, IV or V in the boxes underneath the stave.
Use **one** chord per box.